LEARN HOW TO LEARN

Learn HOW TO Learn

The art of making exams work for you!

MICHAEL MATHEWS

BSc (Cape Town), MA (Oxon)

**with illustrations by
Tony Grogan**

DON NELSON
Cape Town

ISBN 1 86806 046 2
First edition 1988
Second impression 1988

Published by Don Nelson
P.O. Box 859, Cape Town 8000

© Michael Mathews
Illustrations: Tony Grogan
Design: Colleen Goosen
Phototypesetting & Lithographic reproduction:
ProSet-Flexoplate, Cape Town
Printed and bound by: National Book Printers, Cape Town

Also available in Afrikaans under the title
Leer om te leer en presteer met eksamenvernuf!

**We would like to thank Britha Padkin
(BA, UED) for her contribution to the chapter
on speed reading. Britha is actively involved
in two specialised reading and study
improvement courses: KNOW-HOW, a course
ideally suited to scholars, and READ,
(Reading Efficiency and Determination) for
the more advanced readers.**

There is an old story of two University students
who could not decide what to do.
'Let's toss a coin,' said the one.
'If it's heads, we go to the beach,
if it's tails, we go to the movies.
And if it stands on its side, we'll study!'

Contents

Introduction

Today's social and economic environment places ever increasing demands on people to equip themselves intellectually for their rôles in life. Unemployment means that there is greater selection of people for the jobs available and more than ever before, employers are demanding proof of academic achievement. Therefore a higher level of education is required.

It is vital to ensure that you do not lose out in life because of a lack of qualifications. Once you have chosen your career path, it is important to apply yourself immediately to the task of acquiring the necessary qualifications. In fact, long after you have embarked upon your career, it is necessary to keep up to date with new developments. As a result, life is an ongoing process of learning.

If you want to learn anything, it is *entirely up to you*. Nobody can really teach you anything. They can only create an environment in which you might want to learn, and also teach yourself. There are many sources of information available to you: books, films, tapes, records, videos – a whole host of audio-visual aids is at your disposal. It is up to you to make the effort and assimilate or absorb it *yourself*.

In this book we go through the learning process and study techniques step by step, building up from simple basics. In this way you will boost your confidence in your ability to learn, and *confidence* is what you need if you are to be successful in learning and, indeed, in anything you do.

It is a slow but thorough way to demonstrate to you what is necessary to *learn how to learn*. The book is planned so as to illustrate, in its whole presentation, just what your attitude should be towards learning anything.

We focus on several techniques of learning how to:
- concentrate
- speed read
- express ideas and write well
- prepare for examinations
- organise your studies and, therefore
- organise your life.

If you *learn how to learn* the points mentioned above, you will automatically be able to teach yourself how to learn any number of different skills which you might need at some time or other in your life.

What is most important for you to realize is that success rests in the palm of your hand. It is easy to master the techniques but *you* and *only you* will be able to do it.

Sir Isaac Newton was once asked by a man how he discovered the law of gravitation. He replied, 'by thinking about it all the time.' If you think you want to do something and then *determine* and resolve to do it, you can easily accomplish your task. The methods set out in this book will help you to accomplish what you want to do. Practically everything in life today involves *hard work* and determination – the *key to success*.

Just hard work, however, is not enough. You need techniques and strategies. These are set out in this book and the first one we look at in Chapter 1, is how to organise yourself, and how to organise your studies, by *organising your time*.

1. How to organise your time

For a student *time* is an important commodity. Time needs to be *managed* as there are only 24 hours in each day. You cannot rent, hire, or buy more time!

Many of us never learn to manage our time and quite often, when asked how we spent our day, it is difficult to remember exactly how we used our time. It is essential to pre-plan how you are going to allocate your time to the various tasks you have to do.

If you are being examined on six or more subjects you face many tasks clamouring to be done, and you will be effective only if you concentrate on *one task at a time*. If you concentrate, and devote all your attention to *one at a time*, you will get your work done *fast* and *thoroughly*. The more you concentrate time, effort and resources on a single problem, the greater the number and diversity of tasks you can actually perform. But do one thing at a time. If you are studying history do not worry about biology.

SPECIAL STUDY TIME

Your studying should become a *habit* and you must get yourself into a complete routine so that you don't have to think about it. If you ever have

11

to make a decision about whether or not you should study – compared with doing anthing else at all – then almost certainly studying will come second!

(There is an old story of the two University students who could not decide what to do. 'Let's toss a coin,' said the one. 'If it's heads, we go to the beach, if it's tails, we go to the movies. And if it stands on its side, we'll study!')

The great advantage of making a habit of working to a *schedule*, is that you know that if you stick to it you're sure to cover your full curriculum. When exam time comes around, there is no last-minute panic – you will enter the exam room with the confidence that you know your work.

There is also a sense of daily achievement as you work your way through the syllabus. Once you've put in your day's work and accomplished the targets you've set, you will be able to enjoy your leisure time more freely – without any nagging sense of guilt!

How one plans a *work schedule* is discussed in chapter six. Right now we're talking about organising *time*.

HOW TO PLAN YOUR STUDY TIME

Set aside study times each day. Try to be consistent, and devote time to your studies at the same time on each day so that it becomes an easy routine. Work out when the *best time of day* is for you to work. Everyone is different. Some people like getting up early in the morning to work when everything is quiet and your brain and body fresh.

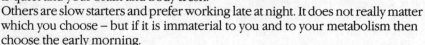

Others are slow starters and prefer working late at night. It does not really matter which you choose – but if it is immaterial to you and to your metabolism then choose the early morning.

The golden rule is to *set yourself a schedule* and stick to it. If necessary, write it out and pin a notice to the outside of your door. Everyone will then become aware that those are your special times for studying and *nobody* should disturb you during these times.

Try going into your room five minutes before your starting time in order to get yourself set up and ready to start on time.

During this 'setting up time' clear your working area of anything that may distract you. Your desk should face a blank wall if possible – if you can see out of a window you will inevitably look out the window; if your desk faces an interesting picture on the wall, you are likely to stare at it and start daydreaming! Keep your time schedule in front of you so that you are reminded of it.

It is vital to get into a well established routine of preparing to work and starting on time. Don't get side-tracked by the telephone, television or people who want to talk.

Because it is impossible to keep concentration up to peak level for a full two to three hours, it is important to take a five-minute break every half-hour. Your work schedule should be so structured that you can work in units. A unit may consist of a particular chapter or section in your syllabus that you are able to cover in 30 minutes of concentrated learning. Then take a complete break and relax for five minutes before tackling the next section. It is better to work at this sort of pitch than to go beyond your best period of concentration. Your absorption rate will then drop markedly and you will not be able to comprehend intelligently.

During this break, get up, walk around, and perhaps do a few exercises. If you are really tired, rather set your alarm, sleep for half an hour, and then get up and focus on the job at hand. Don't feel guilty about the half hour sleep – you needed it, you took it, and now you are refreshed and ready to concentrate.

Some people find that it helps them to concentrate if they have music playing in the background. If this suits you, by all means use this method, but don't play it too loud so that it disturbs others who may find it distracting. If you find yourself listening to it more carefully though, your attention is slipping away from your work and you cannot be concentrating properly.

Learning to concentrate even if there is noise around you is very important. If you can ignore distracting noises such as chairs scraping on the floor or children playing outside or the hubub of university residents, then you will be able to retire into your own cocoon of concentration and will achieve much more in a short space of time.

You will find that good habits learnt now will enable you to achieve much more in life.

As you achieve more, so you will gain confidence. And confidence is one of the great secrets of success. If you believe you can do something, and you organise your time to do it, you will achieve what you set out to do, assuming that you have only very basic skills. Believe that you can do it, and you will. Also, begin with the more difficult tasks and get them done as you will feel so much better that you won't even be tired when you come to the end of that period of work.

HOW TO PLAN YOUR LEISURE TIME
Most people find this pretty easy!

14

The reason for including this subheading is twofold.
Firstly your leisure time must be planned around your work time and you must achieve the right balance between work and pleasure.
Secondly, when you do take time off, *enjoy it*! Do not feel guilty and by all means go to a party, to the beach, to a movie, or play your favourite sport!

POSTURE, LIGHTING AND HEALTHY TONICS

You will only be able to learn if you are fit and well.

When studying, make sure you sit upright in a comfortable position.

Natural light during the day is best for your eyes and at night you should use a blue-coloured 'daylight bulb' of one hundred watt strength.

If you are right handed the light source should be on your left, and vice-versa, so that when you write there are no shadows on the paper.

In addition to healthy eating and regular exercise you may sometimes feel the need for pep-up tonics, and you will no doubt notice the advertising for various tonics as exam times approach.
Ask your doctor or chemist for a vitamin supplement or a tonic with a relatively low caffeine content. Huge quantities of coffee to 'keep you going' are *not recommended*.

2. Learn how to speed read

Every subject requires a large amount of reading. This may become very time consuming if you are a slow reader.

Learning to speed read is a great advantage to any student.

To improve your reading speed just follow these simple, step-by-step methods, do the exercises and you will be able to read much faster – at least 3 to 6 times faster if you wish.

Does that seem incredible to you?

For the moment, reserve your doubts until you have tried it for yourself.

Being able to read fast and to remember what you read is the aim of an efficient reader.

The purpose for this chapter is to show you how to develop your natural ability to read faster with better comprehension and recall. The techniques have been tried and tested over many years and all it needs is your genuine *desire* to save yourself hours of wasted time, having a *positive attitude*, believing you will achieve it, and the will-power to give it a *try*.

As a successful Speed Reader, you will:
- read much more in less time
- improve concentration and sharpen thinking skills
- increase comprehension and become better informed
- develop flexibility and make better use of what you learn
- enjoy becoming more efficient and improving results

ASK YOURSELF THIS QUESTION
Why am I reading this book?

If you have in mind an answer such as wanting to do better, you have already made a positive start. You probably have the motivation to succeed. You must be aware that you *can* do better, or that there must be an easier way, or that you are not  fulfilling your potential in the areas of reading and studying.

Some people are naturally fast readers and seem to read almost as fast as they can turn the pages of a book. Such people are not necessarily 'gifted'. Anyone, even of 'less than average' ability, can learn to improve. The rate at which you read does not depend on an I.Q., or an ability to reason, but primarily on training. Reading is more of a mechanical activity than a creative one. Thus it follows that if reading is a matter of an acquired skill, it can, with practice, be developed and improved.

So why are most people slow readers? Habit. We've been taught that way. We learned the basic mechanics of reading early in Primary school and have been practising reading slowly ever since.

Watch a child who is just learning to read and you will notice he runs his finger along the lines. Why? The reason is that it's the most natural thing to do to help keep the place and focus on the words, allowing the mind to concentrate on what the words mean.

So, just when you were beginning to read more fluently and gaining confidence, your teacher told you to take your finger off the page and read just with your eyes. And that's where your reading development virtually stopped! At that point you began fixing your eyes on every word so as not to lose your place, and were so concerned with 'where's the next word' or 'where's the next line' that your comprehension went down, your confidence went down, and though you certainly read better now than you did then, you still read the same way. This *fixation* habit, one you have been practising ever since, has kept you a slow reader.

Another slow habit that you are probably well aware of is that of having to go back and re-read what you had read because you did not pick up the information the first time. This *regression* is caused by lack of concentration because you were reading too slowly! All unnecessary regression is simply a waste of your time. Surprising as it may seem, comprehension improves with an increase in speed. Concentration picks up and saves you time by not having to keep re-reading. *Vocalising* or saying the words to yourself as you read, even silently, is the third habit which *slows you down*, because you can then read only as fast as you can say the words, at about 200 to 300 words a minute. Sports commentators and auctioneers may get to around 400 words per minute at top speed, and though that might be speed speaking, it is still slow reading.

How do we break old habits? Easy. Overcome them with an easy-to-learn new one. However, it must be remembered that these habits are not wrong in themselves, we can never eliminate them completely, nor is it desirable to do so. For study-type reading of technical or difficult texts, it helps to re-read for better understanding, particularly reading aloud, since we learn better when we employ all our learning faculties of seeing, saying, hearing and writing.

HOW FAST DO YOU READ?

Work it out now. Select a novel, time yourself on a stopwatch, or timer that gives a signal after a set time, or ask someone to time you for 1 minute. Relax and read silently for your normal speed and comprehension. At the end of the minute, stop and count the number of words you have read. This number is your average Reading Speed in words per minute (WPM), in that particular book at that certain time. How did you rate?

Wpm	Rating
below 100	poor
100 – 150	below average
150 – 250	average
250 – 500	above average
600 – 1000 +	Speed Reader

Whatever your starting score, it is far below your capability. Now, how fast would you like to read? It is important to have a definite goal in mind. 3 times your starting speed? 5 times?

Having set your goal rate, let's set about trying to beat your record! We shall now discuss how to overcome the slow reading habits by speed pacing techniques and exercises.

SPEED PACING TECHNIQUES

If you wish to read faster, you obviously need to move your eyes faster. A reading machine will do that for you but it is not always possible to carry around machinery should you need to read fast and effectively. Besides, a machine can merely demonstrate to you how fast you can read. It cannot really train you to do so. You must do that for yourself.

However, you do carry around your own 'equipment' which will do the same trick as a machine. Your index finger. Use your finger as a pacer, like a machine. Having a finger, or pen, pointed at the words on a page, helps to focus attention, improves concentration, and speeds up eye movements. Also, it stands to reason that if you can enlarge your visual eye span to take in 3 words or even 5 words at a time you can read 3–5 times faster.

HOLDING THE BOOK AND TURNING PAGES

Before you begin, hold the book, preferably on a table, in a comfortable position. If your right hand is the pacing hand, then your left hand is placed at the top of the book ready to turn pages as illustrated.

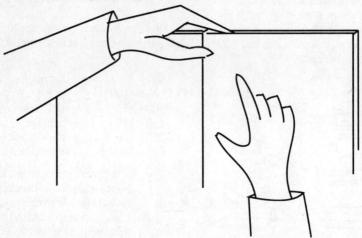

If you are left handed, find a comfortable way of turning the pages with your right hand. Practise for a while to get the feel of just turning pages. Do NOT attempt to read yet.

SPEED PACING TECHNIQUES

At this stage you are just *practising* the basic mechanical hand movement so do *not* attempt to read or try to comprehend. The index finger of your hand is going to sweep across and down the page, from left to right, margin to margin, approximately 10–12 times on each page, as shown on the diagram.

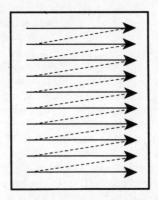

This means with 30 or more lines on a page, you skip every three lines or so. Once you get the feel of the movement, start speeding up. Practise going faster and faster until your hand cannot move any faster.

This speed practise exercise will feel strange at first, after all, this is the first time you've had to 'read' with your arms! You will get used to it and soon develop a comfortable style to suit yourself.

Keep practising for about 3 minutes at a time. Aim to cover about 60 to 70 pages in the 3 minutes. Remember you are not reading, so there will be little or no comprehension at all at first. To start with, all you will see is a blur of print and your hand moving. Keep your eyes watching the page, not your hand or finger, and with repeated practice, out of the blur of words, you will begin to see a few words here and there. Then groups of words will come into focus, and perhaps the general gist of an idea in parts, until later, more and more details will come.

Although it probably feels more like an arm exercise, the *speed pacing technique* is actually speeding up your thinking skills and co-ordinating comprehension at speed. If you repeat this exercise regularly each day, several times a day, you will very soon begin to see the benefits of the method when reading 'ordinarily'.

Remember that all effective speed readers read with a finger or pen as a pacer in all their reading.

Having repeated the 3 minute speed pacing technique several times, let's see how much your actual reading speed has improved. Start at the beginning of your book, or pick up the story where you left off reading. Read again, with the same level of comprehension you had for your first *timed read*, but this time keep your finger moving under the lines as you go. Be prepared to push as fast as you can still understand what you're reading at the time of reading it, even skipping lines if you wish as long as you know more or less what it is about.

Note your starting time and then stop after 1 minute. Next, count up the total number of words you read. You have improved already, haven't you? Congratulations! *You have now become a speed reader!* Now you can see that your goal rate is not so impossible to reach. The reason for your improvement is that your eyes have become conditioned to faster speeds.

SOME HINTS TO MAKE IT EASIER

Once you have mastered the basic hand movement, try a more flexible zig-zag pattern across the page. It is more relaxing, less tiring and allows you to concentrate on what you are seeing.

Try not to count the sweeps once you have developed a rhythm. More or less 10–12 sweeps will do.

Watch the words, not your hand. Think about how they fit together in the context of the story.

It does not matter where your eyes are on the page exactly in relation to your hand. Your eyes will be jumping about, across, and down the page in a natural and relaxed manner as they take in large areas of words at a time. The effect of this exercise is to enlarge your visual eye span so that you can see more words at a time.

Finally, make a constant effort to read faster whenever possible. Set time goals and be determined to get through as much as you can, as fast as you can, and as well as you can in the time set.

HOW TO INCREASE COMPREHENSION AT SPEED

Comprehension means understanding what you are reading at the time of reading it. If you cannot remember it at a later time, it is only that you cannot recall it. Recall is important, but it is a later stage in the reading process, and we will deal with it further on.

Would you say it is essential to read every word to obtain comprehension? No. If you read this sentence:

David boat 10 km shore no fuel clouds wind waves capsized
and if you read this paragraph:

David, having hired a boat for a pleasure cruise, found his fuel running very low while he was still 10 km from shore. Rain clouds had begun to bank up and soon a fierce wind whipped up waves that beat into the boat, eventually causing it to capsize.

It is evident that you have not learned anything new from the paragraph that you did not already know from the key words. Reading word for word is not only unnecessarily slow, but you could lose sight of the whole picture and the enjoyment of the story. At faster speeds your eyes are rapidly 'skimming' over the pages searching for the key words and comprehension comes in the context of the paragraph as a whole.

You might well ask if skimming does not leave out many words or sentences and so you would lose comprehension.

Skimming has a two-fold purpose: You could be going very quickly over the pages to pick up the general idea of the text, as in a preview, or you could be looking for a specific piece of information. In both cases you will not expect full comprehension.

However, with rapid reading, although your eyes will be darting to and fro, they will still pass over and see all the words on the page, and the brain, which has become accustomed to faster speeds, will be able to process the words into meaningful order. Speed reading is *not* for poetry, maths or highly technical formulae. There is a time to speed read and there is a time to read slowly.

COMPREHENSION EXERCISE

1. Preview the book as a whole. The more knowledge you have of the characters, plot and setting, the better your comprehension will be, as you will have a framework on which to build the details.
2. Mark off a section of about 4–5 pages (page numbers) depending on the size of the print. With larger print and fewer words per page, you can take 5–6 pages.
3. Practise rapidly over the whole section in 1 minute to pick up a few words or ideas. Write them down.
4. Read the same section in 2 minutes for more detail. Add to the outline already begun, in your own words if you wish.
5. Repeat the above drill on the next section of 4–5 pages, and so on through the book. If you begin to feel that you know more or less what it is about, extend the section to 6–7 pages in the same time allocations.

RECALL

The ability to remember what we read is extremely important, especially for test purposes. Most of us have experienced the frustration of having read a book and a week later being unable to recall much of it. Equally frustrating is having imformation on the 'tip of the tongue' but being unable to recall it. Faulty recall is due to a lack of concentration, lack of motivation or disorganised thinking.

Psychologists tell us that everything we have read or experienced is registered and retained in the mind. If our brain can be compared to a computer filing system information that is filed in the 'top' drawer or conscious level can be recalled instantly without difficulty. The next level is the sub-conscious level from which we can recall, but not easily. The 'bottom' drawer is the unconscious level and what is retained there is virtually irretrievable.

HOW TO IMPROVE RECALL

For study:

A *positive attitude* will give you the results you want. Believe in yourself and your ability to improve. You *can* if you think you can. Cultivate a genuine desire to remember. If there is a subject you dislike or have no interest in, yet have to remember facts, it is probable that you know very little about it. Go to a library and browse through all the books you can until you discover interesting things which will make it more meaningful for you.

Be *selective*. You cannot expect to read and remember everything that has been written about the subject. Summarising the book to ¼ or less gives you less to learn and you still have all the necessary facts.

When making *notes* use your creative imagination and logical thinking patterns to structure and diagramatise the main points. Memory or recall works by associations and eidetic (picture) images. Notes that are well structured make a dramatic visual impact on the memory. The adage 'a picture is worth a 100 words' is helpful to remember if you wish to improve your recall.

Highlights or fluorescent pens are useful. Use them to establish a bright and attractive colour code eg. blue = aim, green = function, red = result, yellow = conclusion.

Also use a good numbering system to clarify points, or circle words such as 'firstly' or 'secondly'. This method will tie your notes neatly together.

Memory *mnemonic* systems are dynamic aids that help recall because they assist long-term and more permanent recall. Study and apply them at every opportunity.

Discussion groups are particularly helpful for brainstorming ideas on exam questions, difficult sections of the work, or problems in application of theory. 2–4 people is an ideal number for such a group.

GRAPH OF REMEMBERING AND FORGETTING

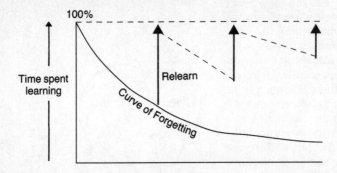

Note that forgetting occurs shortly after learning and if you leave it at that, after a further period of time, most of what you have learned will be forgotten. Initially,

learning new material takes quite a long time, but each time you re-learn, there's less to learn and it takes less and less time. At the end of each week, if you were to set aside *review time* for that week's work, and the end of the month or term, another review time, it is obvious that your recall will be excellent.

VOCABULARY BUILDING

One of the reasons for not comprehending what you read is that you are not familiar with the vocabulary that is being used. In highly technical or unfamiliar subjects, the new terminology and 'jargon' may have no meaning for you, and would result in very poor comprehension. It is essential therefore to *improve your word power*. A good start to solving the problem is to begin with a simpler book and work your way up in the subject.

In the time you spend previewing the book, familiarise yourself with all the new terms, unless there are too many of them, when it would be better to study them chapter by chapter. At least you will not have to break your flow of thought while reading in order to look up a new word. Use a good *dictionary* and even memorise the words and definitions.

It could be that your own knowledge of language is inadequate and you would be well advised to make a daily habit of acquiring and using new words. A most useful and stimulating book for this is a *thesaurus* of synonyms and antonyms which will help you understand and use more words.

FEAR – TERROR –
– DREAD – TREPIDATION
FUNK ALARM – HORROR
CONSTERNATION
DISMAY

THES-
AURUS

English is a rich language with some 490 000 words plus an additional 300 000 technical words. The vocabulary of an 'average person' is only 5 000 words in speech and up to 10 000 words in written communication.

The most famous and complete thesaurus is *Roget's Thesaurus* – started in 1852 by Peter Mark Roget and continually updated and improved.

Try to record all your 'new' words in a small notebook and build up your own dictionary. Also jot down an exciting quote, metaphor, simile or an example of alliteration which will help improve the quality of your writing and expression. Another aid to word building is to learn a list of Latin and Greek prefixes and suffixes, and root word meanings. You will then be able to work out more difficult words and their meanings (see Appendix 3 for examples).

Finally, the more you read, even when the author uses unfamiliar words; as your brain attempts to understand by compensating and substituting other words for that context, the more you will enlarge your vocabulary and improve your comprehension.

HOW TO READ A DIFFICULT SUBJECT OR BOOK

At some time or another, out of interest or necessity, we all have to master a difficult work. If you were to start with the first chapter and work through until you were finished, you would soon get discouraged and feel that you will never complete it. So what is the right approach?

DARWIN
THEORY
OF
EVOL-
-UTION

First the preview. The more important the material or the more difficult the book, the more thorough the preview must be, without getting you bogged down with details and difficulties, and yet it must be quick enough to give you a glimpse of the whole book or section. Study the contents page and general lay-out of the book as a whole.

Then preview each chapter in turn to become more familiar with the terms you will encounter, read footnotes, summaries and questions and study any visual aids.

Do a relatively small section at a time, and work in whole units. For each section, once previewed, jot down headings and subheadings, leaving spaces under each for the amount of detail to be added later.

You are now ready for the *study read*. Using your pencil to pace your eyes along the lines, proceed at a speed that will permit you to understand everything you need as fast as you can. Read the whole chapter in this way, (twice if required) marking important facts as you go. Mark with ticks in the margin, and when re-reading for emphasis, double tick.

Make point-form notes, structuring the information as diagramatically as possible. Review the notes frequently to improve recall and concentration.

PROGRESSIVE READING TECHNIQUES FOR ADVANCED READERS

For senior students who wish to develop their skills further, there are several little aspects to consider, such as flexibility, critical and evaluative reading and how to separate the main ideas and related details from the structure of the text.

FLEXIBILITY

Are you perhaps aware that you have more than just one reading speed?
You do not read a text book at the same speed as you would a novel, nor would you approach it the same way. The more difficult the text the slower you would need to read.
Similarly, when reading a novel, you'll find yourself reading slowly and with greater care over some parts, and you'll almost skim over others.
Flexibility is knowing when to adjust speed and compensate for what you want to get out of the material.

The following *multiple reading approach* will help you discern your purpose and allocate the time you spend on any book or section.

First identify your type of material, your purpose in reading it, and then note the proportion of your time available to be spent on previewing and postviewing.

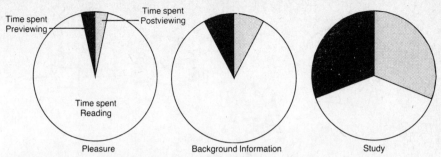

| Pleasure | Background Information | Study |

You will see that the more important the subject matter is, the more time is spent on previewing and postviewing. The advantage of this method is that in previewing for research, you can quickly eliminate what is unnecessary, and it allows you to spend more time on what you have selected. For instance, if you have an hour to study, about 20 minutes will be spent in preparing the section thoroughly, outlining main headings, and studying any visual aids and questions. 20 minutes will be spent just reading, and perhaps marking points, and the last 20 minutes will be for making notes and learning them.

CRITICAL AND EVALUATIVE READING

An efficient reader is a discriminating reader. If you accept that almost everything you read is 'slanted', that it has a bias toward a certain viewpoint, you must learn to read intelligently and critically, or else find yourself gullibly swallowing everything in print as true. Take for example, the range of newspapers and magazines reporting the same news but with totally different aims. Which is to be believed? You must be the judge.

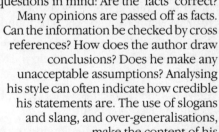

First, consider the author. Study what he says and how he says it. Read with these questions in mind: Are the 'facts' correct? Many opinions are passed off as facts. Can the information be checked by cross references? How does the author draw conclusions? Does he make any unacceptable assumptions? Analysing his style can often indicate how credible his statements are. The use of slogans and slang, and over-generalisations, make the content of his work highly questionable, as does an emotional appeal such as in the 'bandwagon' approach, e.g. 'Everybody buys . . .' or 'It is well known that . . .'

In considering the author's purpose for writing, for whom it is written, and questioning the message of the text, you can soon pick up errors, or deliberate attempts to mislead, and be on your guard against the influences of propaganda.

HOW TO FIND MAIN IDEAS AND RELATED DETAILS

When *previewing*, the main idea is to study the structure and layout of the subject as a whole, so that you can pick out the main points quickly. There are several *directional words* that act as pointers to help you. Those that:

A   Add to the thought
B   Illustrate the idea
C   Compare or Contrast
D   Show Cause and Effect
E   Conclude the topic

A   Words such as *and, also, in addition, furthermore,* indicate that a major statement had just been made and what follows are the details

B   When you read words *for example, like, for instance,* and *such as,* you will realise that the main idea is to be found just before the details that follow on

C   Comparison – *contrast* directional words such as *but, however, yet, similarly, on the contrary,* and they will help you to find the two main statements on either side of them

D   Words such as *because, thus, therefore,* all indicate that one statement results from what has gone before

E   *Finally, thus, consequently,* and *in conclusion,* will clearly indicate when the author is drawing to an end and there may well be a concluding summary statement.

ANALYSING AND SUMMARISING THE CONTENT
AND STRUCTURE OF A PASSAGE

                                                        key words

1. Introduction – gives the general   1. ....   What?
   idea

2. Author's statement about the topic   2. ....

                                            ....   Opinion?

                                            ....

3. Body of facts, figures, observations 3. ....
   and case examples in support of
   statement   ....   Evidence?

                                            ....

4. Conclusion – summary of main   4. ....   Outcome?
   idea

Not all passages are constructed alike as the author's purpose and content matter varies considerably, but there is always a basic form to all paragraphs and essays which you can uncover by asking yourself such helpful questions as:

What is the author's intended message (main theme)?

Why did he write it?

What *type* of literature is it? (descriptive, explanatory, narrative, satirical, serious, humorous)

Has the writer achieved his *purpose*? i.e. how have you responded to the work?

Is it *convincing*?

What effective use of *language* does the author use to create his particular style?

Which words have specially vivid impact as *word pictures*?

Note that these questions for evaluating a passage can be used with equal success on longer works and novels and to be taken into account when writing essays.

REVIEW

Speed reading is one of the most useful, if not essential tools, for your academic progress. Now you have read about reading, and seen an immediate improvement if you tried it out, you're on the threshold of an exciting and rewarding experience, saving time, thinking faster and remembering better.

Always use your hand as a pacer. Research has shown that when you take the pacing hand away, reading rates do drop, but even if that does happen, you will never lose the know how to get back to faster speeds. Skills must be practised to become habits. Just 20 minutes a day will give you amazing results over a few weeks.

Knowing what not to read is almost as valuable as knowing what to read. There is so much that is worthwhile, it is a pity to squander your precious time on unworthy literature. Set goals to help you accomplish your reading requirements and enjoy the pleasure and satisfaction in a world of books which your new reading accomplishment has opened up for you.

3. How to listen and make notes

In the learning process it is obviously necessary to learn to *listen* to teachers or lecturers addressing you and it is important that you concentrate and take good notes. After all, the more you absorb at this stage, the less studying you will have to do later.

Many people attend talks or lectures without taking notes, but this makes it much harder to concentrate. You need never feel embarrassed, even in a public lecture, to have a small note book open and jot down the main thoughts and ideas. Indeed it is a compliment to the speaker, and those people around you who look as though they are concentrating on every word and mentally recording it, are usually only bluffing themselves.

Here are some useful note-taking techniques:

• Learn to write quickly, abbreviate and develop your own shorthand. Some dictionaries have lists of abbreviations that are widely used.

Here are some examples:

ml	millilitre	Fr	French, France
pl	plural	adj	adjective
ch	chapter	p	page
RHS	right hand side	LHS	left hand side

Here are some more personal examples:
therefore ∴   because ∵

• Write the title of the lecture at the top of the page as this will help you *focus* on what the teacher / lecturer is going to say and get into the habit of dating your notes.

• Do not write everything down. Rather try to construct an *outline* of the most *relevant points* and fill in the *main thoughts and ideas*. By concentrating on summarizing and getting an outline down on paper, one can avoid daydreaming. Leave spaces in your outline for any notes you might need to fill in later.

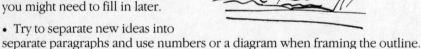

• Try to separate new ideas into separate paragraphs and use numbers or a diagram when framing the outline.

• Watch out for *signal phrases* which *indicate or precede* the central thought of what is said. You can't always write down the actual words as they are spoken but it is important to understand the central theme. Note words or phrases like: 'firstly we want to look at . . .' or 'the aim of . . . ' as this is a great help. Other signal word / phrases are:
– in addition to
– moreover
– further
– finally
– next
– meanwhile
– at last
– for example
– in particular
– to illustrate

Towards the end the speaker will signal with words such as:
– therefore
– in conclusion
– to sum up
– with the result that

- At university you will need to fill out or re-read these notes *each night* before filing them. Your *retention after* listening to a lecture is dramatically lessened over time and, therefore, the sooner you are able to fill in your outline, the better your notes will be. If your notes are complete just glance at them before filing, as you will retain much more over the long term. *Do not attempt to rewrite notes as you will waste valuable time.*

- Often a lecturer will say 'it is not necessary to take notes because I will distribute lecture notes afterwards'. Rather, take brief notes on the central thoughts, and when you collect the written lecture you can fit your pattern outline to it. Go through the hand-out *as soon as possible, underline important sections*, working back to the headings you noted when listening. By using this method, you are able to crosscheck and determine just how well you listened and whether you grasped the central thoughts.

- Another valuable technique is to ask if there is something that you don't understand.
Either interrupt the speaker, (if he/she is happy to take questions during their talk) or jot down the question and make sure that you ask afterwards. If you are embarrassed to ask in front of everyone go personally after the talk and tackle him/her with the question. It is much better to *ask the question* (even if you think it may be a stupid question) than to sit silently and go away with your question unanswered. Often there are a lot of people around you who also don't understand but are afraid to ask the question, and are most relieved when you do. Even if it is a stupid question you will find that 99% of the people who lecture are very happy to explain it again.

- To sum up:
Before you go to a lecture think about the title and what the lecturer is going to say.
If you can look up one or two books on the subject to get a rough idea on the topic, you will be more familiar with it and will gain much more from the talk.

Listen carefully, and actively, and jot down the main thoughts in an outline form as you listen.

Ask questions on any points you don't understand.

Fill in your outline as soon as possible.

This is the ideal way of taking notes, but it is time consuming. When you've had a lot of practice and are adept at taking notes neatly, try to move away from this double work and simply re-read and highlight notes afterwards.

4. How to express yourself

SPELLING

Now that we have covered reading and listening, it is important to concentrate on your ability to express your thoughts clearly and accurately. Numerous words are commonly mis-spelt. Work out a mnemonic or some method to remember the words you have a problem with.

Here are some examples of commonly mis-spelt words:

blame*a*ble	supersede	hypocri*sy*
picnic*k*ing	awkw*a*rd	co*n*jure
shak*a*ble	a*ll*ow	*my*sterious
cushion	di*ss*atisfy	di*s*obey
di*sapp*ear	i*n*oculate	sermon
o*cc*u*rr*ed	pri*vi*lege	coloured
liv*a*ble	scand*a*l	r*hyth*m
su*cc*umb	a*nn*oyance	develo*p*
feasi*i*ble	a*pp*roval	exci*te*ment
rasc*a*l	age*i*ng	hara*ss*
emb*arra*ss	us*a*ge	equi*pp*ed

These examples illustrate how easy it is to work out a mnemonic:
How to remember the difference between *stationary* and *stationery*:

Stationery = writing materials
Stationary = remaining in one place
(Oxford English Dictionary)

If you remember that the 'e' in stationery may represent envelopes then you will never have trouble in spelling the word because you have a mnemonic to indicate the meaning of the word.

How to spell receive, deceive, perceive etc. correctly each time: remember these famous words of advice –
   'i' before 'e' except after 'c' and you will never make the same mistake again!
   There is one exception to the rule: yield

Capitalise the difficult part of the word.
eg parallel – paraLLel
necessary – neCessary
supersede – superSede
argument – arGUMent

Try to *focus on the trouble spots*.
The best method of remembering the difficult words with capitals is to say the words with emphasis on those particular letters.

Another very simple way of helping yourself with spelling is to write the word out ten times. But if you write it out *twenty times* and write it *very fast*, it will really imprint itself on your mind.
Keep a list of your difficult words in a notebook.

If all of these tricks fail, then get a *poster* and put it up in your room or in the bathroom at the back of the door, and write the words that you are having difficulty with in 10 cm high letters so that you can't help noticing them. You could even put one on the *mirror* where you do your make-up or shave so that you always see the word. It won't be long before you can replace it with another. This method also works well when you are trying to learn another language.

To summarise:

Use mnemonics and tricks.

Capitalise the particular letters that are giving you a problem.

Write the difficult ones out 20 times to fix them in your mind.

Keep a list of all your problem words in a note book.

Write out the difficult words on a chart or poster.

WRITING

If you have to sit down and write an essay, here is a quick checklist to run through before starting:

- analyse the question carefully
- how much is required ?
- what are the main points ?
- what is their order of priority ?
- how am I going to group these ideas ?
- additional points of interest
- conclusion

This is a rough outline or plan. Having done this you will have focused on the subject and will have all the valid points in your mind – and it's as easy as that!

A most useful technique is to write the title of your essay in the centre of a page and encircle it. Then jot down other ideas or words at random around the centre circle. If you develop these ideas you will soon have enough to form a logical sequence or pattern for your essay.

Remember : when you write, you are *communicating*. You are writing well if the other person understands what you are saying. For this reason, make sure that you select your words carefully and remember that it is always better to *use simple words* rather than complicated ones. This does not mean that you must not use the *appropriate word* but try to avoid pretentious words, eg use 'begin' instead of 'commence'.

Styles have changed over the years and in your writing you must be *direct* and *simple* and *forthright*. Rather use short sentences than long rambling ones which are difficult to follow.

Don't use – "it is the case that" or "thank you for the letter of the 24th instant" – if it is February, then say "of the 24th February".

READING

Reading is not a passive exercise. It stretches and stimulates your imagination, broadens your general knowledge and your experience of life, and may be enjoyed for any number of reasons. However, as individuals, we all have interests and problems of our own and it is important to read widely so that we might establish which books we really enjoy. If you have access to a library, use it ! Take out books that appeal to you and don't feel obliged to read 'classical' literature if

you're not in the mood
– there's no hurry as
the time will come
when you will *want* to
read them and then
you will probably
absorb much more of
their recognised
worth.

There is no doubt that
reading widely will
improve your
communication skills:

- Your vocabulary will
increase and therefore
your writing will become more expressive.
- Your general knowledge will expand which means that you will begin to read
with more comprehension.
- You will be able to evaluate, analyse and reason with more difficult texts, and
most important of all form your own opinions.

The reading list at the end of the book in Appendix 1 is not exhaustive but includes
an interesting variety of books. Use it as a guide but don't forget your library as it
will offer a great deal of books to suit your immediate interests.

FOREIGN WORDS AND PHRASES
You should only use these *if there is no
suitable English equivalent* but you need
to know their meanings in order to read
fast and avoid regression. Appendix 2
gives you a list of foreign phrases and
their meanings.

COMMUNICATION
Communication involves a *two-way*
process; an exchange of ideas or
knowledge may only take place when
the receiver hears, understands and
perceives *all* that the sender has
intended to convey. Your ability to convey or express your thoughts will require
a good deal of practise. Remember that grammar, punctuation, neat handwriting
and the orderly presentation of your work will improve the communication
process.

5. How to plan for your exams

The secret of organising for your exams is to have a *schedule* and to allocate study time for each subject. You will then find that you get twice as much work done and will enjoy doing it, because you tick off your schedule as the work is completed day by day, and there is a great sense of accomplishment. You will also waste no time in working out your priorities, and then starting on one subject and after half an hour, wondering whether you shouldn't perhaps be doing some other subject!

Firstly make a list of your priority subjects, and estimate how many hours you will need for each one.

Then look forward and assess how much time you will have available on each day and allocate the subjects to suit your times.

Suppose you are going to revise for an exam and you have six subjects.

You are sitting down to make your plan three and a half weeks (25 days) before the exam.

List those days and work out the corresponding hours available.

Your list should look like this:

		TIME AVAILABLE	TOTAL NUMBER OF HOURS
October	Monday 1st	3 – 5pm	2 hrs
		5.30 – 6.30pm	1
		7.30 – 10.30pm	3
	Tuesday 2nd	2 – 4pm	2
		4.30 – 6.30pm	2
		7.30 – 10.30pm	3
	Wednesday 3rd	4.30 – 6.30pm	2
		7.30 – 8.30pm	1
	Thursday 4th	3 – 5pm	2
		7.30 – 10.30pm	3
	Friday 5th	2 – 4pm	2
		5.30 – 6.30pm	1
	Saturday 6th	6 – 8am	2
		8.30 – 10.30am	2
		2 – 5pm	3
		7.30 – 10.30pm	3
	Sunday 7th	8 – 10am	2
		2.15 – 4.15pm	2
		7.30 – 9.30pm	2
			40 hours

You know that you have 40 hours of swotting time available to you. At this stage, deduct 10% of this time for unforeseen problems which may crop up and are unavoidable.

This safety margin of 10% is not because you may miss a study session but *in case you find a section of the work that requires more attention than you thought*. You are left with 36 hours available to divide up over six subjects. (6 hours each). Now work out your priority subjects eg mathematics and English may require, say, only 3 hours each. You therefore have six 'spare' hours to re-allocate to heavy swotting subjects like History.

Now go back to your schedule and allocate the subjects accordingly. Scatter the spare 6 hours evenly through the programme.

October	Monday 1st	3 – 5pm	2	History (2)
		5.30 – 6.30pm	1	English (1)
		7.30 – 10.30pm	3	Geography (2)
				Mathematics (1)
	Tuesday 2nd	2 – 4pm	2	Afrikaans (2)
		4.30 – 6.30pm	2	Spare
				Science (1)
		7.30 – 10.30pm	3	Science (1)
				History (2)
	Wednesday 3rd	4.30 – 6.30pm	2	Geography (2)
		7.30 – 8.30pm	1	Spare

Note: Refer to your 10% safety margin as *spare* and not free!

Once your programme is prepared, get it typed or write it out very neatly and display it on the wall above your desk. Pay strict attention to starting times but if you run over at the end, don't worry! If you are really involved in the subject and have only 6-9 more pages to do to finish a section – spend the extra half-hour on it. Record these additional times however, and if you do more than your allotted 40 hours – so be it! You will have cause to feel good that you

have done *more work* than you had planned, and you deserve to do well in your exam.

Try to complete your programme *before* the start of your first exam. Any available time during the exams should be treated as additional time and you should not rely on it as part of your study programme.

This method of preparing for an exam requires self discipline to make it work – but it is a fantastic system. *Try and make it work for you!*

6. How to pass exams

The only way to pass an exam is to make up your mind on day one of the course, that you are going to pass it, and set your sights on passing it well. Aim high and do your best but, be realistic, and keep a sense of perspective. Doing your best will not only give you a feeling of personal satisfaction but is the only means of ensuring that you achieve your goal. Before starting this section we should recap. In mastering any course ensure that you know *exactly what it is that you have to learn*. You should know your syllabus and have prepared summaries of each section of the work. These should be outlined in your notebook (or on your cards) and when it comes to the end of the year review, you should have the whole course neatly summarised in your notebook, chapter by chapter or section by section. Check through this notebook, analyse your weaknesses and strengths and in doing so you can determine some three or four weeks before the exam just how many hours of revision you will need for each section of the work and, therefore, for each subject overall. The way to plan your time allocations for study purposes is set out on pages 42 and 43, however, what we want to concentrate on here, is how to work at each section.

When you review your work it is not cramming. *Cramming* is the urgent piling up of information in any order at the last minute and it is doomed to failure. It is impossible to store up large quantities of disorganised material, and only if you have the *whole course mapped out* in your mind, you will be able to organise your studies. *For it to be clear in your mind you must have it set out neatly in a notebook*.

Continuous self examination through the year is the best way to prepare yourself for an exam, and the more time you give yourself to prepare, the better you will be able to cope with it. Reduce your course to the *essentials throughout the year* and have those *summaries* set out in your notebook (or on cards) and you will be able to tackle any exam with confidence and success!

PREPARATION FOR THE EXAM
Two steps to take for preparation for that final exam are therefore:

Constant Review Throughout The Year
In the regular reviews through the year always go back to the beginning of the course and quickly glance through everything that you have done up to date and see how it ties in with what you have just completed in a particular week. In this way you become more and more familiar with the work as you progress through it, and in practically all your subjects you will find that there is a thread or *line of continuity* running through the whole course.

Your constant references to the early parts keep them fresh in your mind and make your end of year study much easier. Where you can reduce a chapter to a sentence, do so. This valuable technique will give you a continuous outline of what the course is about (particularly useful in subjects like History and Geography). It is also very helpful when studying a rather difficult section of say, Ancient History or Biblical Studies, to see how each chapter links up with the previous one and how each civilisation is based on certain aspects of past civilisations .

- Continuous weekly reviews keep the older chapters fresh
- Tie in the new chapters
- Give you an overall view of the entire course as it is progressing and, consequently,
- Reduce the amount of last-minute work you need to do.

Final Organisation of your Notebook (or Record Cards)
In the final organisation of your notebook (or cards) you should already have a *main thought outline* of each chapter in the course and of every lecture you have been given in this course. You should also have kept a list of the outside reference reading assignments you have studied, and a vocabulary notebook for the course as a whole. This is particularly useful in the science subjects where definitions and an easy familiarity with difficult words will assist you and give you confidence in tackling difficult questions which are not exact repetitions of the work which you have done during the year. Finally, you should have a separate page listing your weak areas and corrections of common errors.

What you need to do:
- *Make a single outline page for each chapter in the course.* (Many people may prefer to use record cards (15cm x 10cm) and if you have a good filing system this is very much more flexible than a notebook.) In this summary, blend together notes on the chapter itself, on any lectures you have had on the subject, and on any *outside reading*. It is this drawing together of all aspects that gives you your final blending. Each card or each page of your notebook will represent each section of the work and you should then have the whole course set out.
- Study old exam papers, and watch your local newspaper for special features throughout the year. You should have a look at these *during the year* in order to

become familiar with the sort of question the examiners ask, and the way in which they ask them. You can then judge the amount of emphasis placed on each aspect of the course and study the different subjects accordingly. Towards the end of the year work through these papers and try to do them correctly, even if you take longer over them than the time allocated. In a training exercise of this nature, it is important that you write full answers down. In subjects like Maths do not hesitate to seek help from your teacher on any problems you have when doing old exam papers because you are likely to come up with those problems again in your exam.

• As you revise *write down* and *summarise*. If you sit and read you will find your thoughts wandering. The very best method of swotting is to *write things down*. When you tackle a chapter in a textbook, *underline* the important points and *make notes in the margin*. Once you have gone through the whole chapter pull out everything you have underlined and write it down in your notebook or library card. At this stage you will find that the summary is still quite long, so eliminate all unnecessary words and phrases and write the whole thing down again. If you constantly keep yourself writing, underlining and picking out all important points or highlighting them with coloured pens, you are constantly making yourself *focus on the important points* and you achieve much more than you would by just reading.

You will find:
that the time goes very quickly;
your concentration improving
and that you don't get bored or sleepy;
work more satisfying
because you *know* that
you have mastered it.

• Remember to put difficult sections of the work on a *big poster*. Draw bold, colourful diagrams, display them in various places, and memorize the posters so that when you are in an exam you will be able to reproduce it exactly.

Don't leave the same poster up for too long – replace it with the next subject. But keep them all and just before the exam, *put them all up!*

- You must learn to work, underline and make notes *fast*. Keep your notes *neat* so that you can read them the next time round but the main emphasis should be on *speed*. In this way one never becomes disillusioned about the quantity of work to do.

- *Set yourself questions*

When you prepare for an internal exam in a school or University, try to set the exam by putting yourself in the teacher's shoes. Inevitably you will be able to guess 80% of what the teacher will eventually ask you if you set yourself two quite separate exam papers, each covering the work. Having done that, work through those questions in outline form only (always remembering that you must do so as quickly and as accurately as possible) and you will be very *well prepared* for the exam.

This should also apply to essays in subjects such as English and Afrikaans literature. It is always useful to have a few descriptive sentences or paragraphs up your sleeve that you have worked on and polished and can then reproduce in an exam. However, this does not necessarily apply to creative writing. You should be careful not to put all your emphasis on spotting exact titles – rather select *sections* of the work or very broad and general titles. In essay work this is, of course, particularly dangerous because *you must answer the question*.

Parrot learning and narrow spotting can get you into a *lot of trouble and cause panic. Well thought out preparation*, putting yourself in the teacher's position, having good quotations and descriptive phrases which you can feed into essays will score extra marks for you in the exam.

47

If you get short one-word-answer type questions or a multiple choice paper, then setting yourself an exam is a good exercise. You can always combine the *work with a friend* and you can prepare one chapter and the friend the next, thus alternating throughout the book. Doubling up will help to achieve a balanced questionnaire in half the time. Set the questions, wait a day or two and then do your answers and correct the work immediately. Write out and highlight the correct answers to any of your errors and *learn* them. At this point discussion helps one to learn because you combine several study techniques and at the same time you learn to express yourself clearly, you say the correct answer aloud and you have to concentrate.

There is nothing more satisfying than sitting down in an exam room and finding that the questions on the exam paper are the ones that you were anticipating, that you were wanting, and that you know all about.

You are, of course, only half-way there if you know the questions, but if you have done your preparation properly and if you have *written out the answers*, you will know them too.

You will start the exam full of *confidence*, and will be able to tackle any questions that are included to test your *thinking* ability on the subject because you will be well prepared in the *overview and understanding* of the course as you are in its detail.

Remember that if you have a choice of questions that may be answered in any order, you should *always do your best question/answer first*.

Watch the time and divide it up proportionately.

You should possibly give the first answer considerably more time than you will devote to the last. If you have to answer 3 questions in three hours, then divide the time into 75, 60, and 40 minutes, leaving yourself with five minutes grace for finishing off an answer. It may seem strange to allocate so much time to question 1, but it is often worthwhile to show the examiner that you really have *mastered* at least one of the questions.

If you are thoroughly familiar with your work and have researched the sort of questions that you could be asked, you should never be confronted with a type or form of question that you cannot answer.

Thorough preparation is the key to *success*.

You must be able to respond to the challenge and will certainly be rewarded for your effort.

To sum up then:
- Prepare and master the content of everything in your course.
- Become familiar with the type of question that you will be asked.
- Practise.

IN THE EXAM ROOM

The first thing to do when you look at an exam paper is to read through the instructions and make sure that you understand *how many questions have to be answered*. When you read a question through, read slowly and *underline anything that is important*.

eg Answer *three* out of the first *five* questions and then *two* out of the following *four*. Draw a line on the exam paper after question 5 and write boldly in the margin 3/5. Alongside the next group write 2/4.

Read and re-read carefully and if there is any doubt at all ask the invigilator or examiner. In a multiple choice paper, don't forget to check whether you are required to tick or cross the answers. Try to work out the answer before working through your alternatives as they may confuse you. Otherwise, select the correct answer by a careful process of elimination.

If you have to answer questions in a specific order then make sure you do so, but if not choose your *best question first*.

Ration your time.

Before you start a question plot the outline of your answer if it is an essay type question. This step is vital if you are going to answer the question clearly.

When tackling an essay *underline the key words* in the question and always remember to relate back to the question throughout the essay. The final paragraph should always start with the question or a concluding phrase. Following this, try to tie together the main points of your argument or assessment of the question.

Too many people read a history question for example, and say to themselves, 'Ah, the Unification of Germany,' and the people who just write on the unification of Germany, do not answer the question properly. The question may have been: 'To what extent did the Customs Union bring about the Unification of Germany or would it have come about in an event as a result of Prussian leadership in other spheres?' This sort of question does indeed require a full survey of the steps leading up to the Unification of Germany but *emphasis* must be placed *where the examiner wants it* to be placed.

It is essential to underline the key words in the question and to ensure that at the very least, in your opening paragraph and in your final paragraph you make direct reference to the question. If you are aware of this you will inevitably bear it in mind throughout the essay. Of two essays with the same facts, the one that answers the question and places the emphasis where it should be is the one that will score the highest marks.

Pay particular attention to key words in the question such as:
   evaluate, outline, compare, explain, criticise, name, discuss, list, define, state, review, describe, enumerate, illustrate, interpret, justify, prove, contrast.

Be sure to do exactly what is required. If you are asked to 'list' then 'list' – don't give an outline or a criticism.

In the more involved questions where you have to take a stand, make sure that you come out positively in support of one or other argument. An example of this type of question is 'Did Charles I deserve to lose his head?' You can and must always put the case for both sides but *make your own position clear* and support both with facts. Do not be too bold or extreme in your opinions in a language essay or poetry critique or in a subject such as History, where emotions, political opinions or religious thoughts may be involved. It is seldom that the examiner will ask a one-sided question and it is important to *strike a balance* throughout the essay and be fair in setting out an argument or counter argument. You are being tested on your knowledge of a subject and on your philosophy of the subject in academic terms. You are not usually being asked for your own political or religious thoughts. Strong bias could influence the examiners attitude and whilst you should not be afraid to express your ideas you should do so in a reasonable and responsible manner – you will achieve more this way. It is not advisable to overstate a case or support a point of view very strongly or emotionally.

If you find that you have some time over at the end of an exam, try to rack your brains for extra points to add to your answers. Use an asterisk and write a note asking the examiner to turn to the last page for a further point. Only if you are confident that you have every relevant point should you start reading through and polishing your essay answers.

Always keep some time at the end to check calculations for careless mistakes. It is estimated that people lose about 20% of their marks through careless errors. The way to avoid these is to know where they occur. Here are some examples:
• People fail to answer the question properly and they miss the meaning of key words.
• They read only part of the question.
• They don't obey instructions.

If you find that time is running out and you have judged it badly *don't panic*! Tackle the last question even if you only have 5 minutes in which to do so. If it is an essay type question simply jot down as many of the facts as you possibly can.

Do so neatly so that the examiner can read them and organise them into paragraphs just as you would an outline. You may get a friendly examiner who will give you some credit for knowing something even if you have not had time to put it down in essay form. Even 20% on that last question is better than 0!

When you go into an exam room try to *keep calm* and read the paper slowly and carefully. Ignore the various antics of your friends – many of whom raise eyebrows, draw in their breath and generally make a big fuss when they first see their papers. This is not going to help you and you haven't time to grin or do anything else but concentrate, so get on with it quietly and in your own way. *Shut yourself off* in your own little world and start plotting!

Make sure that this step-by-step approach towards exams becomes second nature to you. Working regularly does require self-discipline, but the will to succeed and a positive attitude will provide all the motivation and drive you need. We are all capable of achieving *the full extent of our potential*. No one can ask more of you than that!

Appendix 1

RECOMMENDED READING LIST

The following reading list does not pretend to be complete. It will introduce you to some of the world's most interesting authors. In most cases, only one book has been listed against each author and this is not always the book for which the writer is most famous. Once you have 'discovered' an author it is also easy to find other books of the same genre.

There is such a wealth of 'good' material to read that you should derive great pleasure from reading. Reading will broaden your knowledge and experience of life as well as improve your expression. In order to write well you need to learn from other people's experiences, their style, and their way of perceiving and portraying the world.

Don't forget to consult your librarian if you have difficulty in finding these books and become familiar with your catalogue.

Ancient World
Homer
Plato
Aristotle
Aeschylus
Sophocles
Euripides
Lucretius
Virgil
Marcus Aurelius

Middle Ages
St. Augustine
Chaucer, Geoffrey
Dante (Alighieri)
Omar Khayyam

Plays
Chekhov, Anton
Goethe, Johann Wolfgang von
Ibsen, Henrik
Molière
Shaw, George Bernard

Poetry
Blake, William
Coleridge, Samuel Taylor
Donne, John
Yeats, William Butler

General Literature
Balzac, Honoré de
Bunyan, John
Cervantes, Miguel de
Dostoyevski, Fyodor
Flaubert, Gustave
Hugo, Victor
Tolstoy, Leo
Voltaire
Zola, Emile

Classics from the 18th and 19th Century
Austen, Jane   *Pride and Prejudice*
Brontë, Charlotte   *Jane Eyre*
Brontë, Emily   *Wuthering Heights*
Carroll, Lewis   *Alice's Adventures in Wonderland*
Conrad, Joseph   *The Secret Agent*

Defoe, Daniel   *Robinson Crusoe*
Dickens, Charles   *Great Expectations et al.*
Dumas, Alexandre   *The Three Musketeers*
Eliot, George   *Middlemarch*
Fielding, Henry   *Tom Jones*
Forster, E.M.   *Passage to India*
Hardy, Thomas   *Tess of the d'Urbervilles*
Kipling, Rudyard   *Kim*
Melville, Herman   *Moby Dick*
Pepys, Samuel   *Diary*
Shelly, Mary   *Frankenstein*
Stevenson, R.L.   *Treasure Island*
Swift, Johnathan   *Gulliver's Travels*
Twain, Mark   *Huckleberry Finn*

20th Century Classics
Adams, Richard   *Watership Down*
Alcott, L.M.   *Little Women*
Bach, Richard   *Johnathan Livingstone Seagull*
Bellow, Saul   *Humbolt's Gift*
Blixen, Karen   *Out of Africa*
Burgess, Anthony   *Clockwork Orange*
Camus, Albert   *The Outsider*
Clavell, James   *King Rat*
Dahl, Roald   *Kiss Kiss*
Doctorow, E.L.   *Ragtime*
Douglas, Lloyd C.   *The Robe*
Durrell, Lawrence   *The Alexandria Quartet*
Fitzgerald, F. Scott   *The Great Gatsby*
Gallico, Paul   *The Snow Goose*
Galsworthy, John   *The Forsyth Saga*
Golding, William   *Lord of the Flies*
Grahame, Kenneth   *Wind in the Willows*
Green, Graham   *England made me*
Haley, Alex   *Roots*
Heller, Joseph   *Catch 22*
Hemingway, Ernest   *For Whom the Bell Tolls*
Heyerdahl, Thor   *Kontiki*
Huxley, Aldous   *Brave New World*
Irving, John   *The World According to Garp*
Joyce, James   *Ulysses*
Kafka, Franz   *The Trial*
Lawrence, D.H.   *Sons and Lovers*
Lee, Harper   *To kill a Mocking Bird*

Maugham, W. Somerset   *Selected short stories*
Mitchener, James   *The Drifters*
Munthe, Axel   *The Story of San Michele*
Nabokov, Vladimir   *Lolita*
Orwell, George   *Animal Farm*
Pasternak, Boris   *Dr Zhivago*
Rand, Ayn   *Atlas Shrugged*
Sewell, Anna   *Black Beauty*
Sholokov, Mikhail   *And Quiet Flows the Don*
Steinbeck, John   *Of Mice and Men*
Stowe, Harriet Beecher   *Uncle Tom's Cabin*
Tolkien, J.R.R.   *Lord of the Rings*
Tossler, Alvin   *Future Shock*
Verne, Jules   *20,000 Leagues under the Sea*
Waugh, Evelyn   *Brideshead Revisited*
West, Morris   *The Devil's Advocate*
Wilder, Thornton   *The Bridge at San Luis Rey*
Woolf, Virginia   *To the Lighthouse*

Modern Light Novels

Adams, Richard   *Maia*
Anthony, Evelyn   *No Enemy but Time*
Archer, Jeffrey   *A Matter of Honour*
Atwood, Margaret   *Life before Man*
Bartel, Constance   *A Woman Like That*
Binchy, Maeve   *Firefly Summer*
Braine, John   *A Room at the Top*
Christie, Agatha   *Murder on the Orient Express*
Clavell, James   *Whirlwind*
Cronin, A.J.   *The Citadel*
Daly, Janet   *The Pride of Hannah Wade*
du Maurier, Daphne   *Rebecca*
Durrell, Gerald   *My family and other animals*
Farre, Rowena   *Seal Morning*
Forsyth, Frederick   *The Day of the Jackal*
Freeman, Cynthia   *A World full of Strangers*
Green, Kate   *Shattered Moon*
Hartley, L.P.   *The Go-Between*
Irving, John   *Cider House Rules*
Jaffe, Rona   *Mazes and Monsters*
Le Carre, John   *The Perfect Spy*
London, Jack   *White Fang*
Marsh, Ngaio   *Photo-Finish*
Maxwell, G.   *Ring of Bright Water*

Mitchell, Margaret   *Gone with the Wind*
Monsarrat, Nicholas   *The Cruel Sea*
Mortimer, Penelope   *The Pumpkin Eater*
Robbins, Tom   *Still Life with Woodpecker*
Salinger, J.D.   *The Catcher in the Rye*
Seton, Anya   *Katherine*
Shaw, Irwin   *Rich Man, Poor Man*
Sheldon, Sidney   *Windmills of the Gods*
Shute, Nevil   *A Town like Alice*
Smith, Stevie   *Over the Frontier*
Stuart, Mary   *The Ivy Tree*
Theroux, Paul   *The Mosquito Coast*
Uris, Leon   *Exodus*
Walker, Alice   *The Color Purple*
Wallace, Irving   *The Prize*
Weldon, Fay   *The Hearts and Lives of Men*
Wilkerson, David   *The Cross and the Switchblade*

African Literature
Abrahams, Lionel   *The Path of Thunder*
Achebe, Chinua   *Things Fall Apart*
Ayi Kwei Armah   *The Healers*
Bosman, Herman Charles   *Mafeking Road*
Brink, André   *An Instant in the Wind*
Cloete, Stuart   *Rags of Glory*
Coetzee, J.M.   *Life and Times of Michael K.*
Cope, Michael   *Spiral of Fire*
Dikobe, Modikwe   *The Marabi Dance*
Du Plessis, Menán   *A State of Fear*
Fitzpatrick, Sir Percy   *Jock of the Bushveld*
Fugard, Athol   *Tsotsi*
Gordimer, Nadine   *A Sport of Nature*
Head, Bessie   *A Collector of Treasures*
Joubert, Elsa   *The long journey of Poppie Nongena*
Khuzwayo, Ellen   *Call me Woman*
Lessing, Doris   *The Grass is Singing*
Marais, Eugene   *The Soul of the White Ant*
Matthee, Dalene   *Fiela's Child*
Ngugi Wa Thiong'o   *Petals of Blood*
Oesmane, Sembene   *Gods Bits of Wood*
Paton, Alan   *Cry, the Beloved Country*
Poland, Marguerite   *The Bush Shrike*
Rive, Richard   *"Buckingham Palace", District Six*
Rooke, Daphne   *Mittee*

Schreiner, Olive   *The Story of an African Farm*
Smith, Pauline   *The Beadle*
Soyinka, Wole   *The Interpreters*
Wilhelm, Peter   *Some place in Africa*
Van der Post, Laurens   *The Lost World of the Kalahari*

Booker Prizewinners since 1970

1970 Bernice Rubens   *The Elected Member*
1971 V.S. Naipaul   *In a Free State*
1972 John Berger   *G*
1973 Stanley Middleton   *Distractions*
1974 Nadine Gordimer   *The Conservationist*
1975 Ruth Prawer Jhabvala   *Heat and Dust*
1976 David Storey   *Saville*
1977 Paul Scott   *Staying On*
1978 Iris Murdoch   *The Sea The Sea*
1979 Penelope Fritzgerald   *Offshore*
1980 William Golding   *Rites of Passage*
1981 Salman Rushdie   *Midnight's Children*
1982 Thomas Keneally   *Schindler's Ark*
1983 J.M. Coetzee   *Life & Times of Michael K.*
1984 Anita Brookner   *Hotel du Lac*
1985 Keri Hulme   *The Bone People*
1986 Kingsley Amis   *The Old Devils*
1987 Penelope Lively   *Moon Tiger*

The CNA Literary Award

1970 John McIntosh   *The Stonefish*
1971 Jack Cope   *The Rain-maker*
1972 Sheila Fugard   *The Castaways*
1973 Alan Paton   *Apartheid and the Archbishop*
1974 Nadine Gordimer   *The Conservationist*
1975 Guy Butler   *Selected Poems*
1976 Anthony Delius   *Border*
1977 J.M. Coetzee   *In the Heart of the Country*
1978 André P. Brink   *Rumours of Rain*
1979 Nadine Gordimer   *Burger's Daughter*
1980 J.M. Coetzee   *Waiting for the Barbarians*
1981 Nadine Gordimer   *July's People*
1982 André P. Brink   *Chain of Voices*
1983 André P. Brink   *Looking on Darkness*
1984 J.M. Coetzee   *The Life and Times of Michael K*
1985 Douglas Livingstone   *Selected Poems*
1986 Ellen Khuzwayo   *Call me Woman*
1987 David Robbins   *The 29th Parallel*

Appendix 2

Foreign words and phrases should be used only when there is no satisfactory English equivalent. Since the main purpose of your writing is to communicate, you should use simple words wherever possible. The purpose of this list is to give the meanings of foreign phrases that you may come across in your reading. There is no suggestion that you should try to use them yourself.

SELECTED FOREIGN WORDS AND PHRASES

ad infinitum	*without limit*
ad nauseam	*satiated to the point of disgust*
aide memoire	*aid to the memory; memorandum*
à la carte	*only those items selected from the menu are to be paid for*
Alma Mater	*one's old school or university*
alter ego	*a second self; an intimate friend*
a posteriori	*from effect to cause; inductive*
a priori	*from cause to effect; deductively*
au fait	*familiar with*
au revoir	*until we meet again*
bête noire	*bugbear; pet aversion*
bon voyage	*pleasant journey*
bona fide	*in good faith*
carte blanche	*full powers*
cause célèbre	*a lawsuit that arouses considerable interest*
consensus	*agreement (in opinion)*
contretemps	*an unlucky event; a mishap*
coup de grace	*death blow*
coup d'état	*sudden overthrow of a Government (by force)*
de facto	*in fact*
de jure	*in law; by right*
denouement	*outcome (of event); solution (of difficulty)*

en masse	*in a body*
en route	*on the way*
errata	*list of printers' errors*
ex gratia	*out of thanks; an act of grace*
ex officio	*by virtue of (his or her) office*
extempore	*without previous study or meditation*
fait accompli	*accomplished fact*
gratis	*free*
hoi polloi	*the masses*
incognito	*with one's identity concealed*
in toto	*in total*
ipso facto	*in the fact itself; automatically*
magnum opus	*one's greatest work*
maître d'hôtel	*head steward*
mala fide	*in bad faith*
métier	*one's calling or trade*
modus operandi	*mode of procedure*
mutatis mutandis	*after making the necessary changes*
née	*born*
noblesse oblige	*rank has its obligations*
nonpareil	*of unequalled excellence*
nuance	*subtle shade of meaning*
pari passu	*in an equal proportion*
Poste Restante	*to be left at the Post Office until called for*
post mortem	*occurring after death*
pro rata	*in proportion to*
quid pro quo	*one thing in place of or in return for another; compensation*
R S V P/(répondez s'il vous plaît)	*please reply (usually to an invitation)*
sic	*appended in brackets after a word or expression to denote that it has been quoted correctly although its incorrectness or absurdity might suggest that it had been wrongly quoted*
s'il vous plait	*if you please*
sine die	*indefinitely*
sine qua non	*indispensable condition*
sotto voce	*in an undertone*
status quo	*existing state of things*
stet	*let it stand*
sub judice	*said of an undecided case before a Court of Law*
subpoena	*a summons to attend a Court of Law*

table d'hôte	*meal at a restaurant or hotel for which a fixed price is paid irrespective of the number of courses taken*
terra firma	*firm or solid earth*
vade mecum	*a pocket book; a book of reference*
vide	*see*
vis-à-vis	*face to face*
viva voce	*by word of mouth; oral*

Appendix 3

PREFIXES AND SUFFIXES

Listed here are common Latin and Greek prefixes and suffixes which are used very widely in English. If you learn five a day, you will improve your vocabulary. This will also help you to increase your reading speed.

PREFIXES

Front part	Meaning	Examples
a	*not without*	atypical, aseptic
ab, abs	*to free from*	absolve, abdicate
ad	*to change (direction or by addition)*	adhere, advocate
amb, ambi	*about, around, both*	ambiguous, ambivalent
amphi	*both, around*	amphibious, amphitheatre
ante	*before*	anteroom, antecedent
ant, anti	*opposed to*	anti-labor, antacid

Front part	Meaning	Examples
arch, archi	*chief, principal*	archbishop, archipelago
aut, auth, auto	*self*	automatic, automobile
bi, bis	*two, double*	biennial, biped
caco	*bad, ill*	cacophonous, cacography
circum	*around*	circumference, circumnavigate
cis	*on this side of*	Ciskei
col, com, con	*jointly*	combine, collate, conjunction
contra	*against*	contradict, contrary
counter	*in opposition to*	counteract, counterplot
de	*from, down, concerning*	deduce, debar
di, dis	*away from*	dismiss, dissect
dia	*between*	dialogue, diameter
epi	*upon, on, over*	epitaph, epigram
equi	*equal*	equidistant, equilateral
ex, e	*out*	exit, expel
extra	*beyond, outside of*	extraordinary, extracurricular
hetero	*another, different*	heterogeneous, heterodox
homo	*same*	homogeneous, homonym
hyper	*over*	hypercritical, hyperbole
hypo	*under, below*	hypodermic, hypochondriac
im, in	*not*	inept, imperfect
inter	*between*	interstate, intertwine
intra	*within*	intrastate, intravenous
intro	*place before*	introduce, introvert
mal, male	*bad*	malpractice, maladministration
meta	*after, change*	metaphor, metaphysics
mis	*wrong*	mislable, misnomer
miso	*hatred of*	misogyny, misogamy
mono	*one, alone*	monologue, monoplane
multi	*many*	multiply, multinational
neo	*new*	neophyte, neolythic
non	*not*	nonsense, non available
ob	*against*	obstruct, object
ortho	*correct, right*	orthoptic, orthodox
pan	*all*	panacea, panchromatic
para	*beside*	parallel, paragraph
per	*through*	permit, perennial
peri	*around*	perimeter, peripatetic
poly	*many*	polygon, polysyllabic
post	*after*	postscript, posthumous
pre	*before*	prejudge, prevent
pro	*before*	pronoun, progress

Front part	Meaning	Examples
proto	*first*	protocol, prototype
pseudo	*false, fictitious*	pseudopod, pseudonym
psycho	*relating to mind or soul*	psychology, psychosis
re	*back, again*	reincarnation, rearrange
retro	*back, backward*	retrospect, retroactive
se, sed	*away, aside, apart*	secede, sedition
semi	*half*	semi-circle
sub	*under*	submarine, suburban
super	*above*	superabundant, supernatural
syn	*together*	syntax, syndicate
trans	*through, across*	transport, transcend
tri	*three*	triangle, trimaran
ultra	*excessive*	ultra-modest, ultra conservative
un, uni	*one*	uniform, unique
vice	*in place of*	vice versa, vice consul

SUFFIXES

End part	Meaning	Example
able, ible	*characterised by*	illegible
age	*state*	marriage
al	*belonging to*	constitutional
an, ain	*a member of*	Republican
ance	*quality*	abundance
ancy, ency	*quality or state of*	clemency
ant, ent	*one who does*	servant
ar	*relating to*	angular
ard, art	*one who does*	coward
ary	*engaged in*	secretary
ate	*to make*	animate
ation	*the act of*	supplication
cy	*practice of*	democracy
dom	*state of*	martyrdom
ee	*one who receives*	consignee
eer	*one who is engaged in*	volunteer
en	*to make*	hasten
ern	*belonging*	eastern
er	*one who does*	footballer
ery	*occupation*	monastery
esque	*like, style of*	statuesque
ferous	*bearing, giving*	auriferous
fold	*number*	manifold
ful	*full of*	wishful
gram	*a writing*	telegram
graph	*a writing*	autograph
hood	*state of*	motherhood
ial	*pertaining to*	editorial
ic, ical	*resembling*	fantastic
ice	*act, quality*	justice
ify	*to make*	mollify
il, ile	*capable of being*	versatile
ine	*of the nature of*	canine
ion	*the act of*	decision
ious	*full of*	ambitious
ish	*characteristic of*	bookish
ism	*state of*	fascism
ist	*one who practices*	communist
ity	*quality of*	acidity
ive	*tending to*	abusive
ize, ise	*to follow an action*	economise

End part	Meaning	Example
less	*lacking*	useless
ling, long	*showing direction*	headlong
logy	*study of, science of*	biology
ly	*having qualities of*	friendly
ment	*act or process of*	investment
ness	*a quality*	happiness
or	*one who does*	spectator
ose	*containing*	verbose
ous	*full of*	mountainous
ry	*practice of*	carpentry
sion, tion	*the act of*	ascension
trix	*feminine agent*	executrix
tude	*state of*	servitude
ty	*practice of*	fidelity
ure	*act of*	rapture
vorous	*feeding on*	omniverous
ward	*direction of*	eastward
wise	*way of*	clockwise
wright	*maker*	playwright

Finally, here are some of the root words themselves:

Root Word	Meaning	Example
acer, acr	*sharp*	acid
ag, act, ig	*carry on*	agency
ali	*nourish*	alimentary
ali, allo, alle	*other*	alias
alt	*high*	altitude
ambul	*walk*	amble
am, em	*friend*	amicable
amo, ama	*love*	amorous, amity
anim	*life*	animation
annu, enni	*year*	annual
anthrop	*man*	anthropology
appe	*a call upon*	appeal
aqua, aque	*water*	aquatic
arbiter	*a judge*	arbitration
art	*art*	artistic
ast, astr	*star*	astrology
audi, aur, aus	*hear*	audible
bell	*hostile*	rebellious
bible	*book*	bibliography
bio	*life*	biology

Root Word	Meaning	Example
brevi	*short*	abbreviate
cad, cas, cid	*fall*	cadence
cam, chamb	*room*	chamber
cant, chant, cent	*sing*	cantata
ced, ceed, cess	*go*	recede
celer	*speed*	accelerate
cent	*hundred*	century
chief, cap	*head*	captain
capt	*take, seize*	capture
chrom, chromo, chroma	*color*	panchromatic
chron, chrono	*time*	synchronize
cide, cis, cise	*cut, kill*	suicide, scissors
cit	*arouse*	excite
civ, civi	*citizen*	civic
clam, claim	*shout*	clamour
clud, cluse	*close, shut off*	exclude
cline	*bend*	recline
coc, coct	*cook*	concoct
col, cul	*till*	cultivate
cor, cord	*heart*	accord
corp, corps, corpor	*body*	corporation
cras	*tomorrow*	procrastinate
cred, creed	*believe*	incredible
cresc, crue, cret, crete	*grow*	increase
crux, cruc	*a cross*	crucifix
crypt	*hide*	cryptogram
culp	*guilt*	culpable
cur, course	*to run*	concurrent
cur, cura	*care*	curate
cycl	*wheel*	cycle
deca	*ten*	decade
dem, demo	*people*	democracy
derm	*skin*	epidermis
dexter	*right-handed*	dexterity
di, dia	*day*	diary
dic, dict	*speak*	dictate
dign	*worthy*	dignitary
doc, doct	*teach*	doctrine
dom	*master*	dominate
dom	*house*	domestic
dorm	*sleep*	dormitory
du	*two*	duet

Root Word	Meaning	Example
dur	*hard, lasting*	durable
duc, duct	*lead*	educate
dynam	*power*	dynamic
err	*wander, go astray*	errant
erg	*work*	energy
ego	*I*	egotist
fac	*do*	factory
fer	*carry*	transfer
ferv	*boil*	fervent
fid	*faith, trust*	fidelity
fil	*son*	filiate
fin	*limit*	final
frim	*strengthen*	affirm
flex, flect	*bend*	flexible
flu, flux	*flow*	fluent
fort	*strong*	fortress
fract, frang	*break*	fragile
frater	*brother*	fraternity
fug	*flee*	fugitive
gam	*marriage*	bigamist
gen	*birth*	gender
geo	*earth*	geography
gest, ger	*carry*	gestation
gov, gub	*govern, rule*	government
gress	*walk, go*	progress
graph	*write*	autograph
grat	*pleasing, agreeable*	gratitude
grav	*heavy*	gravity
greg	*crowd*	congregate
hab, hib	*have, hold*	habit
homos	*same*	homonym
hydr	*water*	hydrant
ject	*throw*	reject
jud	*right*	judgment
junct, jug	*join*	junction
juven	*young*	juvenile
labor	*toil, work*	laboratory
laud	*praise*	laudatory
lav	*wash, clean*	lavatory
leg, lig, lect	*read, choose*	legible
leg	*law*	legislature
lib	*book*	library

Root Word	Meaning	Example
liber	*free*	liberty
liter	*letter*	literal
loc	*place*	location
locu, loqu	*speak, talk*	elocution
log	*word*	dialogue
luc, lum	*light*	illuminate
lud, lus	*play*	allude
magn	*great*	magnify
mand	*order*	mandate
man, manu	*hand*	manual
mar, mari	*sea*	maritime
mater, matr	*mother*	maternal
matur	*ripe*	mature
med	*middle*	median
men, ment	*mind*	demented
mens, mest	*month*	semester
merg	*dip*	submerge
meter	*measure*	diameter
mis, mit	*send*	permit
mon	*advise*	admonish
morph	*shape*	amorphous
mor, mort	*death*	mortal
mov, mot, mob	*move*	remove
mut	*change*	mutant
nasc, nat	*born*	nativity
nihil	*nothing*	annihilate
nom, nomin	*name*	nominate
nov	*new*	novice
nym	*name*	pseudonym
oper, opus	*work*	operator
path	*feeling*	sympathy
pater, patr	*father*	paternal
parl	*talk*	parliament
ped, pod	*foot*	pedal
pel, puls	*drive*	impulse
pend, pens	*hang, weigh*	impending
pet	*seek, ask*	petition
petr	*rock*	petrify
omni	*all*	omnibus
phil	*love*	philosophy
phobia	*fear*	hydrophobia
phon	*sound*	telephone

Root Word	Meaning	Example
plic	*twist*	complicate
poli	*city, state*	political
port	*carry*	portable
pot	*power*	potentate
prim	*first*	primary
pris, prehen	*seize, grasp*	apprehend
prob	*test*	probation
put	*think*	compute
pyr	*fire*	pyromaniac
rog	*question*	interrogation
reg, rec	*direct*	direct
rupt	*break*	rupture
sci, scio	*know*	conscience
scop	*watch*	telescope
scrib, script	*write*	describe
seg, sect	*cut*	section
sed, ses, sid	*seat*	session
sens, sent	*feel*	sentiment
sequ, secu, suc	*follow*	sequence
sol	*alone*	solitude
solv, volu	*loosen, free*	absolve
somin	*sleep*	insomnia
soph	*wise, wisdom*	sophomore
spec, spect, spic	*look, see*	spectacle
spir, spirit	*breathe*	aspire
spond	*promise*	despond
sta, sti, sist	*stand*	circumstance
stead	*plac*	steadfast
strict	*bind*	district
stru	*build*	structure
tact, ting	*touch*	tactile
tang	*touch*	tangible
tend	*extend*	extend
tena, tain	*hold*	detain
tent, tempt	*try*	attempt
term	*end, limit*	terminal
terr, ter	*earth*	inter
tele	*afar*	telescope
theo	*God*	theology
therm	*heat*	thermometer
tor, tort	*twist*	distort
tract	*draw*	tractor

Root Word	Meaning	Example
trib	*pay, grant*	tribute
typ	*model*	typical
umbr	*shadow*	umbrella
urb	*city*	urban
val	*strength*	validity
ven, vent	*come*	convene
ver	*true*	veracity
vert, vers, verse	*turn*	divert
via, voy, vio	*way*	convey
vinc, vict	*conquer*	victor
vir	*man*	virile
voc	*call*	vocation
vol	*wish*	voluntary
volu, volv, volt	*turn, roll*	involve
zoo	*animal*	zoology

Summarising

The following summaries are written out in full. Remember that you may shorten these with your own abbreviations and with the aid of diagrams, you can simplify them even further! Once you get into the habit of summarising, this process will become second nature to you. Constant practice enables one to pick up key words and ideas quickly, and a large quantity of work will no longer seem as daunting bcause you will be able to memorise it easily.

If you were to summarise this book for yourself, it is possible that your summary might look quite different and you may have placed greater emphasis on certain points. Do not worry! If you have thought about the content of the chapter clearly, there will be a logical reason for your interpretation and if you are able to explain or substantiate this, then you are on the road to success. The idea is to understand and to simplify the work for yourself!

SUMMARY OF THE INTRODUCTION

Why is the process of learning and education so important?
• rising unemployment figures.

• social and economic pressure.

• the business world is competitive.

• higher levels of education are required.

How do I learn how to learn?
• start with a positive, determined attitude.

• realise that learning is entirely up to you.

• learn successful step-by-step techniques so that you boost your confidence.

• use all sources of information available, eg library, audio-visual aids.

SUMMARY OF CHAPTER ONE

How to organise your time
- manage your time effectively.

- work out priorities.

- establish a schedule.

- concentrate on one task at a time.

- work fast and thoroughly.

Advantages
- no last-minute panic and cramming!

- you will boost your confidence and achieve a good balance between work and pleasure.

Practical suggestions
- prepare your working environment for study.

- warn people that you are intending to study – they are less likely to interrupt you.

- make sure that your desk is at the right height.

- don't slouch!

- avoid eye-strain: use adequate light.

- work in half-hour units and take a break after each one.

- while working: try to ignore distracting noices eg scraping chairs, and if music in the background helps – fine, but don't let it disturb others.

- During your break: relax or exercise, and sleep if you need to.

- eat healthily!

SUMMARY OF CHAPTER 2

How to speed read:

Learning is time consuming if you are a slow reader.

Facts about reading
- reading is an acquired skill.

- training and practice is required for improvement.

Fixation: the habit of fixing your eyes on every word so as not to lose your place.

Regression: going back to re-read what you have read due to a lack of concentration.

Vocalising: saying the words to yourself as you read.

How to overcome slow habits
- Learn how to hold a book and turn pages.

- use the Speed Pacing Technique and speed up thinking skills, and co-ordinating comprehension at speed.

- a more flexible zig-zag pattern may be used once the basic hand movement has been mastered.

How to increase comprehension at speed
- by reading word for word you lose sight of the concept of the passage.

- skimming helps one to pick up a general idea of the text, or to select a specific piece of information quickly.

Recall (the ability to remember)
- faulty recall is due to a lack of concentration and motivation or disorganised thinking.

- everything we read is retained at a conscious, subconscious or unconscious level.

- one may recall from the conscious level without difficulty.

How to improve recall
- cultivate a genuine desire to remember.

- be selective and summarise.

- make 'creative' notes with dramatic visual impact.

- use colour codes, numbering and underlining.

- work out mnemonics.

- activate discussion groups.

- review your work each week.

How to read a difficult subject or book
1. preview.
2. 'study read'.
3. make notes in point form and use diagrams.

Flexibility: knowing when to adjust your reading speed according to the material and your purpose for reading it.

Critical and evaluative reading
- watch out for a 'slanted' viewpoint, bias and propaganda.

- Evaluate by previewing (analysis of the structure and layout of the subject) and noting directional words.

- Also, ask yourself questions to help clarify the text.

Conclusion
- speed reading is an essential tool for academic progress.

- always use your hand as a pacer.

- knowing what not to read is almost as valuable as knowing what to read.

- one may derive much pleasure and enjoyment from reading.

SUMMARY OF CHAPTER 3

How to listen and make notes

Listening
- improves concentration
- helps you to understand and select the most significant points
- makes one aware of signal phrases

Note-taking techniques
- learn how to write quickly and legibly
- use abbreviations
- don't try to write everything down
- construct an outline and fill in main thoughts and ideas
- concentrate on layout: use clear paragraphs and diagrams
- underline or highlight significant sections

Ask questions!

Do not rewrite notes. Rather spend time reviewing, to improve recall, and summarising.

SUMMARY OF CHAPTER 4

How to express yourself

Spelling

Methods of remembering difficult words:
- work out mnemonics and rhymes.

- focus on trouble spots and emphasize or capitalise difficult letters.

- write the word out twenty times to fix it in your mind.

- make a chart or poster and stick it up in an obvious place.

Writing
- make a rough outline or plan before you start.

- develop ideas in a logical sequence.

- keep your style and wording simple and direct.

Reading
- stretches and stimulates imagination.

- should be enjoyed.

- use the library.

Foreign words and phrases
- learn these to avoid regression.

Communication
- a two-way process.

- an exchange of ideas that will only take place when the receiver hears and understands all that the sender has intended to convey.

- to improve this process: write neatly and express yourself clearly.

SUMMARY OF CHAPTER 5 AND 6

How to plan for your exams
- draw up a detailed timetable.

- analyse your weaknesses and strengths.

- be realistic.

- don't try to fit too much into your schedule.

Cramming doesn't work!

Preparation during the year
- constant review and summarising.

- organisation of notes and sections.

- use record cards, charts and posters.

- study old exam papers and special exam features in your newspaper.

Final preparation
- work neatly.

- work with speed.

- set yourself questions.

- don't try to learn everything.

- discuss work with friends.

Make up your mind that you are going to pass and pass well!

In the exam
- be confident, keep calm and do your best.

- read instructions very carefully.

- read through the whole paper first.

- select your questions and plot an outline.

- underline key words and thoughts

- always refer back to the question.

- time yourself well.

Remember that success requires hard work and self-discipline. A positive attitude will provide all the motivation and drive you need.

We are all capable of achieving the full extent of our potential!

EXAM TIMETABLE

Days of the week:	Fill your time available in here:	Subjects / Sections to be studied:
Monday		
Tuesday		
Wednesday		
Thursday		
Friday		
Saturday		
Sunday		